MARK ALVAREZ
writer / editor

MARK RUCKER
concept / design / pictures / research

TOM SHIEBER
writer / research

Let's begin by reviewing the official rules of baseball: "Rule 1.01-Baseball is a game. . . ." STOP! We needn't read further. Baseball is a *game*. Baseball isn't greedy owners or overpaid players or labor strikes or lockouts or agents or lawyers. Baseball is a game. Don't believe us? Turn the pages, look at the pictures, and read about the game of baseball . . . for the fun of it.

* *

Pick it up. With your eyes closed, on the darkest night, you know what it is. Grip it in your fingers. Feel the seams. Throw it your way. Catchers snap from the ear. Second basemen flip sidearm. The big motion is for pitchers. Outfielders take their crow-hop and come straight over the top.

Two pieces of leather sewn with 216 stitches around a cork center and two rubber cushions (one black, one red) wound with wool yarn. Spun in tricky slants by crafty portsiders. Fired who knows where by fuzzy-cheeked flamethrowers looking for the plate. ("He could throw it through a brick wall," they said of Rex Barney, "if he could hit the wall.") Slapped at by pugnacious hustling little infielders, hammered deep by muscled sluggers. Notoriously dropped by Snodgrass and Owen. Famously caught by Mays and Rice (the umpire said so, anyway, and so did Sam in the note he left us). Bounced wonderfully—shades of Babe Herman, who always claimed it actually hit him on the shoulder—off Canseco's noggin.

Machine-signed by league presidents and personally autographed by every pro—once, astonishingly, at no charge. Rubbed pre-game by undershirted umps with Lena Blackburne's mud. Tossed disdainfully back by pitchers looking for higher seams and a bigger edge. Caught off the screen by barehanded batboys. Prized for a lifetime by lucky bleacherites.

Tossed wildly or whacked ("I didn't know I could hit it that far.") through windows by legions, generations, of horrified youngsters (is there any more awful sound or fearful feeling?). Curved around poles to persuade doubting (and obviously non-playing) physicists. Caught on the bat by Rizzuto and rolled to precisely the right spot.

Sped dazzlingly around the laughing circle by the Gashouse Gang. Rolled gently to the mound by the rising catcher after an inning-ending whiff, or fired to third at other times with no one on. Making the paunchy base coach (remember when he was young and stick-thin?) dance comically out of the way. Hopping over Lindstrom's shoulder or into Kubek's throat. Dying in Ozzie's glove. Ricocheting off Maz's hands to first.

Dampened by Big Ed Walsh and grizzled, grandfather-claused Burleigh Grimes. Also—less openly (or maybe not)—by subsequent slippery masters like Gaylord Perry. Made to fade by Matty and The Meal Ticket, two giants of the game. Taught to dive by Sutter but forked earlier by Elroy. Responding as ordered after an earnest conversation with the Bird.

Elegantly hammered by Junior and The Kid. Snapped quick like a rocket by DiMag and Molly. Sent into orbit—over roofs, through windows, into gardens and parking lots and playgrounds—by the Babe and Jimmie, Josh and the Mick. Their children, bigger and bigger, bashing on.

Our perfect icon, symbol to us of fleet (and fleeting) youth. Of good times, of happy days. The spheroid, the pill, the horsehide, the old apple. The baseball.

Let's play.

It's July 6, 1954, and Sal Maglie celebrates yet another victory at Ebbets Field. With a 5-2 decision over Brooklyn, the Barber improved his record to 10-0 against the Dodgers in Flatbush, and 21-7 against them overall. Three weeks later Maglie's streak of wins at Ebbets Field finally ended, but the Giants would go on to win the pennant and World Series.

The authors would like to thank the following for their generous help: Miwako Atarashi, Carlos Bauer, Philip Block, Larry Gerlach, Liane Hirabayashi, Robert Klein, Larry Lester, Jerry Malloy, Andy McCue, Mom, Dan Ross, Jay Sanford, Staff at the Los Angeles Amateur Athletic Foundation Paul Ziffren Sports Resource Center, and Bob Tiemann.

Ralph Terry smiles as he affectionately displays the ol' apple. He wasn't smiling in the fall of 1960 when he gave up Bill Mazeroski's Series winning homer, but two years later Terry once again found himself pitching Game Seven of the October classic. That time he held on for the win and grabbed Series MVP honors to boot.

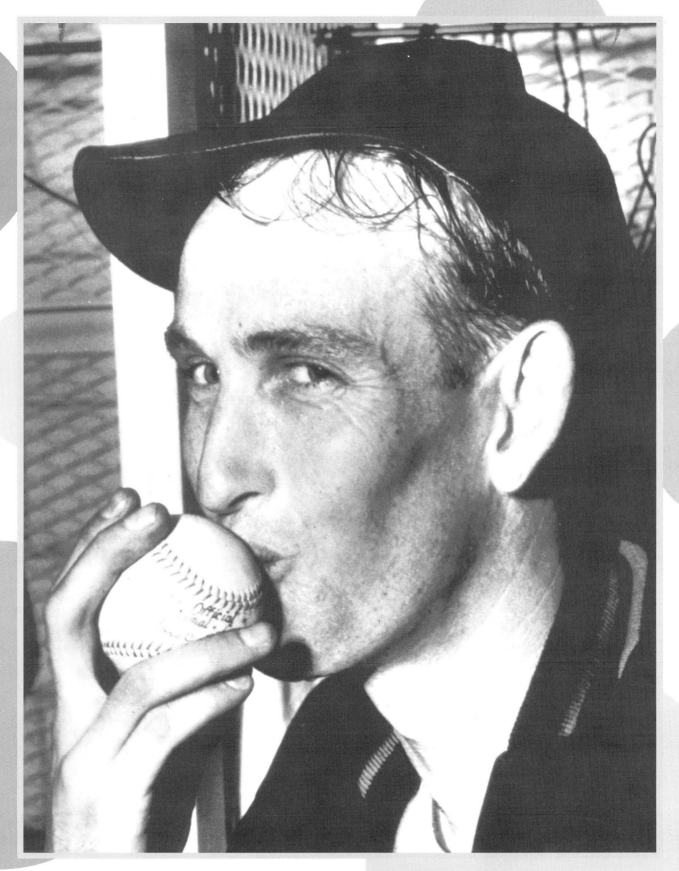

A side-armed phenom from San Dimas, California, Ewell Blackwell strung together a sixteen game winning streak during the first half of the '47 season. His eighth straight victory came on June 18: a no-hitter against the Braves. After the game he paid tribute to the orb with a kiss. Prior to his next start, "The Whip" audaciously predicted a second consecutive no-hitter and managed to hold up his end of the bargain until Dodger Eddie Stanky singled up the middle with one out in the ninth. After the game Blackwell reflected: "I just stood there looking at that ball, that little white ball lying on the grass."

A picture's worth a thousand words. Thank goodness it's so, 'cause Steve Carlton (left) never said more than a dozen. It's obvious Lefty enjoyed batting practice, and it paid off too. When the Phils captured the NL East flag in '78, the only teammate to top Carlton's .291 batting average was Larry Bowa at .294!

"Keep your eye on the ball!" Whether it's batting or fielding, those are the watchwords of every baseball coach. The Red Sox keystone combo of Don Buddin and Chuck Schilling (facing page, upper right) are fixated on the ball as they cover second during spring training in Scottsdale, Arizona, 1961. In Lakeland, Florida, longtime Grapefruit League headquarters of the Tigers, coach Joe Cusick employs a pop-up machine to train prospective Tiger catchers (facing page, bottom). And above at the A's camp in Ft. Myers, Florida, Al Benton (left) and Bill Dietrich (right) help Pinky Higgins with his juggling act.

Still have your eye on the ball? Cleveland second-sacker George Strickland does as Chico Carrasquel works the DP against the A's Hector Lopez, 1956. Note the sparse crowd in the left field bleachers at Municipal Stadium—despite the Indians' second place finish, '56 was the first season since the end of the war in which Cleveland failed to draw at least a million fans.

Frank Frisch took spring training seriously, as did his mentor John McGraw. The Fordham Flash (below, left) shows a rookie how to execute the shovel toss in spring training, c. 1924. Some forty years later, Frisch would remark: "Today's ballplayers are spoiled. . . . Take the way these boys suffer through spring training. They live in country-club surroundings. They swim, play golf, lounge on the beach, and about two or three hours a day play a little ball."

In action from an All-American Girls Baseball League game in 1947, South Bend Blue Sox first baseman Marnie Danhauser stretches for a high throw as Marie Mahoney of the Racine Belles safely reaches first. In the background, Rita Briggs of the Peoria Red Wings leaps and snags an oversized ball. When the league began in '43 the regulation AAGBL ball was 12" in circumference. Over the years, league rules changed (always toward a game more similar to that played in the big leagues) and by 1954, the gals were playing with the same 9-1/4" ball that the major leaguers tossed around.

The ball that these Yanks are so skillfully tossing around is none other than a Reach Official American League Ball with "the cushioned cork center." Over the years Reach made dozens of different kinds of baseballs, each with its own distinctive name: the Bounding Rock, the Sky Scraper, the King of the Field, the Cock of the Walk. Spalding countered with the High Flyer, the Rocket Ball, and the Eureka. But as Reach was owned by A.G. Spalding and Brothers, the supply of balls to most every organized league was monopolized by the giant sporting goods conglomerate.

This montage of dancing Yankee infielders shows (left to right): Gerry Coleman whipping the ball to first while levitating above a sliding Dale Mitchell (Frank Umont makes the call as Phil Rizzuto looks on); Clete Boyer ducking to avoid Tony Kubek's throw; Billy Martin tossing to first to complete a twin killing, and, in a rare stint at shortstop, Clete Boyer leaping for an errant catcher's throw as the Tigers' Bill Bruton steals second. Note the fielder's glove lying in the grass in the Billy Martin photo. The practice of leaving one's leather in the field while your club was up to bat was commonplace until it was outlawed in 1954.

The debate over the origins of the grand old game of baseball have raged for over a century. In 1905, sporting goods magnate and former ball playing star, Albert Spalding, jingoistically declared that "baseball was a natural evolution from the old colonial game of 'One Old Cat.'" As Spalding professed, One Old Cat eventually became Two, Three, then Four Old Cat, Town Ball, and finally Base Ball. Spalding's version of pre-history contradicted that of Henry Chadwick, who steadfastly argued that baseball grew out of the English children's game of

rounders. Al quickly dismissed rounders as nothing more than the "first cousin to that other juvenile pastime of 'Drop the Handkerchief'"—never mind that Chadwick had been covering baseball games well before Spalding even finished grade school.

These staged versions of Town Ball (above) and Four Old Cat (below) were photographed for use in Spalding's history of baseball, *America's National Game*.

On wooden floors, frozen ponds, and wide open fields, baseball has been played most everywhere. Why, believe it or not, nowadays they even play on plastic grass!

And you thought the Polo Grounds had a short left field porch? Indoor baseball began in Chicago in 1887, but quickly spread east. In this *Harper's Weekly* woodcut from 1890, members of the local militia play ball in the 13th Regiment armory at Brooklyn. (Thomas Edison had perfected the electric light bulb only a decade before.) By the turn of the century, indoor baseball was so popular it had its own official ball and its own official rule book (right). The Hydrants, seen below, were a champion indoor baseball club, c. 1910.

CONSTITUTION, BY-LAWS
AND
PLAYING RULES
OF THE
ASSOCIATION
OF
INDOOR BASE BALL
CLUBS

1896

PUBLISHED BY THE
AMERICAN SPORTS PUBLISHING COMPANY
241 BROADWAY, NEW YORK
Copyright, 1896, by American Sports Publishing Company

Baseball was played in Colorado more than a century before the big leagues broke into the rarified air of Denver. On facing page bottom, the Rockies (the mountains, not the Blake Street Bombers) provide a stunning background to an 1889 ballgame at Estes Park, just 50 miles northwest of the Mile High city.

Baseball on ice was first played in western New York state in the early 1860s, but soon the craze made its way to the big city. The first game on ice played between clubs from the New York metropolis was scheduled for January 24, 1861. It was snowed out! A week and a half later, in front of a crowd of some twelve thousand spectators, the Charter Oaks of Brooklyn and the champion Atlantics of Bedford met on the ice at Litchfield's Pond in South Brooklyn. The game allowed for ten men to a side, the extra fellow acting as a second catcher to stop passed balls from otherwise endlessly skidding to the banks of the pond.

Over a dozen years later, the game was still played on rinks throughout Long Island. This January 1884 *Harper's Weekly* woodcut depicts action from a match played at the Washington Skating Park in Brooklyn. A professional team headed by Billy Barnie defeated an amateur club handpicked from local schools by none other than Henry Chadwick.

As one might expect, the rules of baseball on ice differed from those of regular baseball. For example, the ball was pitched underhand to the batter, never thrown. And the base runners (or, shall we say, base skaters) were allowed to overskate each base, not just first, as long as they curled off to the right after passing over the "bag" (a 3 by 3 foot square drawn on the ice).

Little League baseball was born in 1939 when Carl Stotz helped organize three ball clubs (Lycoming Dairy, Lundy Lumber, and Jumbo Pretzels) for young boys in Williamsport, Pennsylvania. Fifty years later, Little League baseball could boast that nearly three-quarters of all major leaguers had at one time played ball in the kids' circuit. Today, Little League ball is tightly woven into the fabric of baseball.

At left are two competitors from the 1962 Little League World Series held at Little League Park, Williamsport (below left). In the final game that year, a 6'1'' 210-pound 12-year-old named Ted Campbell walked the first batter he faced and then pitched six perfect innings, leading San Jose, California, to victory over Kankakee, Illinois.

Few recall that over twenty-five years before the birth of Little League ball, a baseball league for kids under the age of eleven was active for a number of years in Little Rock, Arkansas. The Ne-Hi (or Knee-Pants) League was first organized by a Mr. V.C. Balding in 1913 and fielded teams such as the Microbes, Midgets, Dingers, Dwarfs, and Cats' Ankles. According to the 1915 *Reach Baseball Guide*, "originally, eight clubs were in the league, but the 'Babies' lost a string of games and the older boys in the neighborhood one day caught them, made them suck milk out of a two gallon bottle, removed their breeches and put gunnysack didies on them, wheeled them around the bases in an old baby buggy, to show them how to get around and otherwise mistreated them, and they refused to play thereafter."

Baseball has given us numerous ballplaying brothers. A trio of Wright brothers (Harry, George, and Sam) all wore red stockings for Boston in 1876. And, on September 15, 1963, for one inning against the Pirates, the San Francisco Giants outfield was comprised of nothing but Alous: Felipe, Matty, and Jesus. The Cardinals' Cruz brothers, the Boyers of rural Missouri, the incomparable DiMaggios, and (deep breath) Ed, Frank, Jim, Joe, and Tom Delahanty–the diamond has seen its share of siblings. But, an entire club made up of brothers? Yes, indeed. Presenting the Stenzaks of Waukegon, Illinois. Posed (left) in 1922, the All-Brother champions planned to defend their title against the Marlett Brothers of Hawk Springs, Wyoming. The outcome of the family feud is a mystery.

Below is the Ingvolstad family baseball team of Colorado Springs, yet another club that evidently followed the "play together, stay together" motto.

Au jeu! Little is known about the baseball nine pictured below, though it is probable that these fellows were members of a turn-of-the-century club from Quebec.

Different countries, different languages, same game. Baseball has been played practically everywhere: from Sri Lanka to Venezuela, Australia to Finland, Namibia to Ukraine.

Suishu Tobita, Japan's "god of baseball," once said: "Baseball is more than just a game. It has eternal value. Through it, one learns the beautiful and noble spirit of Japan." Take that, Jacques Barzun!

The photo below shows action from the 1927 Inter-Middle School Baseball Championship Tournament. In this quarterfinal game, Waseda Jitsugyo played Aichi Shogyo at Koshien Stadium in Nishinomiya, near Osaka. The ballpark, now known as Hanshin Koshien Kyujo, was built in 1924 and is currently home to the Hanshin Tigers of the Japanese Central League.

On October 15th, 1933, just a week after the Giants defeated the Senators in the World Series, Lefty O'Doul and Joe Cronin returned to their native San Francisco where both winner and loser were treated to a hero's welcome. As the Municipal Band played "California Here I Come," the pair paraded up Market Street to the Civic Center, where they were mobbed by their young admirers. Later that day at Seals' Stadium, O'Doul, Cronin, and a host of major league all-stars played a charity game against the top players from the Pacific Coast League. Close to $5,700 in profits went to a Christmas fund for needy families. By the way, the PCL squad beat the major leaguers, 5-3, with an 18-year-old rightfielder named Joe DiMaggio going 2-for-2 against the big leaguers.

"Every boy likes baseball, and if he doesn't he's not a boy." —Zane Grey.

"Every boy likes baseball, and if he doesn't he's not a boy." —Zane Grey.

To hero worshipping boys, these Giants really were giants. Left, David Hawkey, a three-year-old fan from Phoenix, poses with New York hurler Jim Hearn at spring training, 1956. Above, Cliff Melton and little Eddie Rapp prepare to catch a ball at the Giants training camp in 1940. At nearly six and a half feet in height, Melton regularly dwarfed his teammates, let alone little kids.

Teammates with Kelly for four years, Old Hoss Radbourn was as cantankerous as Kelly was jovial. At right, Rad has a little fun in the studio as both his bat and his middle finger (left hand) are carefully posed.

Cap Anson described King Kelly (left) as "a whole-souled, genial fellow, with a host of friends, and but one enemy, that one being himself. . . . He was as good a batter as anybody, and a great thrower. . . . He was a good fielder when not bowled up, but when he was he sometimes failed to judge a fly ball correctly, though he would generally manage to get pretty close in under it. In such cases he would remark with a comical leer: 'By Gad, I made it hit me gloves, anyhow.'"

Rube Waddell (above) always was a bit askew. As Jimmy Austin recalled, "Rube was just a big kid, you know. . . . It was always just a game with Rube. He played 'cause he had fun play- ing, but as far as he was concerned it was all the same whether he was playing in the Big Leagues or with a bunch of kids on a sandlot. The main thing you had to watch out for was not to get him mad. If things were going smoothly and everyone was happy, Rube would be happy too, and he'd just go along, sort of half pitching. Just fooling around, lackadaisical, you know. But if you got him mad he'd really bear down, and then you wouldn't have a chance. Not a chance. Hughie Jennings, our manager at Detroit, used to go to the dime store and buy little toys, like rubber snakes or a jack-in-the-box. He'd get in the first base coach's box and yell, 'Hey, Rube, look." Rube would look over at the jack-in-the-box popping up and down and kind of grin, real slow-like, you know. Yeah, we'd do everything to get him in a good mood, and to distract him from his pitching."

In 1922, after toiling in the minors for ten years, Dazzy Vance (above) finally made it to the big leagues for good. He was 31 years old. Over the next decade, no pitcher would win more major league games than "the Dazzler." Here he is in May of '25 showing off fifty $20 gold-pieces, his reward for being named National League MVP of 1924. Dazzy's black armband was worn in memory of Charles Ebbets. The longtime owner of the Dodgers had passed away about a month before this photo was taken.

John McGraw called spitballer Bugs Raymond (right) "one of the greatest natural pitchers that ever lived." In other words, while Bugs was at times unhittable (he once hurled back-to-back no-hitters in a minor league doubleheader), he was otherwise uncoachable. His problem was an unquenchable affinity for the sauce. Hans Lobert: "Oh I remember Bugs. I told him one time (I batted against Bugs and he had the best spitball I ever batted against), I says, 'You don't spit on the ball.' I says, 'You blow your damn breath on the ball and the ball comes up drunk!'"

McGraw, who wasn't shy of signing troubled ballplayers, tried in vain to corral Bugs' drinking problem. The Giant manager once hired a detective to shadow Raymond for a day and report back all that had occurred. In a mock trial, McGraw read the detective's report: "Your operative followed one Bugs Raymond for eighteen hours and noted his every movement. At 9 am the said Raymond went into a saloon known as the Turf Exchange. In a back room he drank seven glasses of beer, ate a handful of pretzels and two Bermuda onions. From there your operative followed the said Raymond to the Knight saloon. There he drank nine glasses of beer, ate more pretzels and two or three onions." The report continued in this vein at length. Upon completion of McGraw's reading, Raymond was livid: "Of course, I might've had a coupla dozen glasses of beer, but I'm tellin' you it's a lie—I ain't eat an onion in seven months!"

Supplement to the NATIONAL POLICE GAZETTE, No. 1663, Saturday, June 26, 1909.

ARTHUR RAYMOND.
One of the Leading Box Artists of the National League who Has Greatly
Strengthened the New York Giants in the Pitching Department.

In 1912, it looked as if injuries and plain old aches and pains would sideline
Hughie Jennings (above right) from the coaches box. Fearing the loss of the
colorful Detroit manager, Grantland Rice lamented as only he could:

REQUIEM OF THE LINES

THERE'S A HUSH ABOVE THE BATTLEFIELD, A LULL ABOVE THE GREEN;
A BODING SILENCE TRICKLES ON THE ONE-TIME GIDDY SCENE;
THE BASE HIT ECHOES LOUDLY AND THE THUD OF FLYING FEET
RESOUNDS ACROSS THE PASTURE WITH ITS OLD SONOROUS BEAT;
BUT OF WHAT AVAIL, THESE NOISES WHEN IT GATHERS TO THE TEST
WHERE THE E-YAHS CEASE FROM BUBBLING AND THE WHISTLE IS AT REST?

THE GAME MAY GROW IN SPLENDOR WHERE THE RAVING ROOTERS ROAR,
AND THE TUMULT LEAP IN VOLUMES AT THE TIEING OF THE SCORE;
THE VOCAL CATACLYSM MAY UPLIFT THE REELING ROOF
WHEN SOME BOLD AND HARDY TOILER SKIDS IN BLITHELY ON THE HOOF;
BUT I KNOW OF ONE, MY BROTHERS, WHO WILL MOURN THE ANCIENT ZEST
SHOULD THE E-YAHS CEASE FROM BUBBLING AND THE WHISTLE LIE AT REST.

Whether it was in front of a ballpark crowd or a camera lens, Babe Ruth was always the main attraction. The Babe was willing to do practically anything for the photographers who followed him everywhere, and the cameramen were often rewarded with great shots. Here's the Bambino during his first year with the Yankees, smoking a cigar and fishing in Central Park.

It had been years since the last time Portland had seen snow, but when the Babe visited the great northwest in December of 1926 (below), the weather obliged and the Sultan of Swat was given a new kind of "ball" to sign.

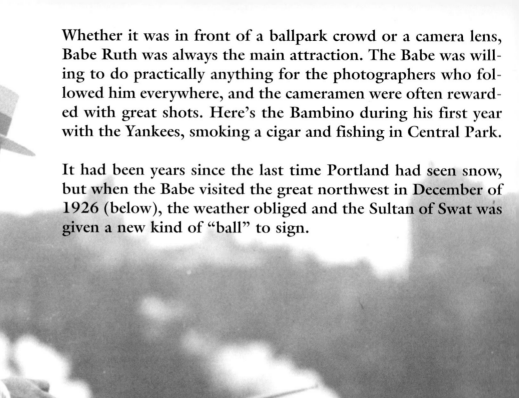

EITHER WAY

WHEN RUTH, THE MIGHTY SOCCANEER,
STANDS UP TO SOCK THE BALL,
THE THRONG IS BOUND TO RAISE A CHEER
NO MATTER WHAT BEFALL.
IT THRILLS THE VAST AND NOISY CROWD
TO SEE A FOUR-BASE CLOUT,
AND YET THE CHEER IS JUST AS LOUD
WHEN SOME ONE STRIKES HIM OUT.

—AUTHOR UNKNOWN, 1921.

When New York purchased Ruth from the Red Sox, Ping Bodie expressed concern over his position in the Yankee outfield: "I suppose this means I'll be sent to China." Instead, it was Sammy Vick who was the odd man out. Indeed, not only did Ping pair up with Ruth and Duffy Lewis to form the 1920 Yankee outfield, but he even ended up rooming with the Babe or, as the story goes, the Babe's suitcase. Above are Ping and Babe at training camp in '20, no doubt discussing the long ball. With Boston the season before, Ruth clouted a major league record 29 home runs, but that was one shy of the total that Bodie socked back in 1910 for the San Francisco Seals. Of course, those long Pacific Coast League seasons provided Ping with more than two hundred games in which to swing for the fences.

In 1920, following a devastating fire at St. Mary's Industrial School for Boys, Babe was eager to help rebuild his alma mater. In an effort to raise money, Ruth spent part of the season escorting the school band around the country. Here's Babe and the band at Shibe Park, Philadelphia, before a showdown with the Athletics.

Babe was more than happy to pose with an ape (above), but *call* him an ape and it was a surefire invitation for a fight.

In 1930, Babe put on an Indian headdress and hammed it up for the camera (right). Little did Ruth realize that five years later he'd be swinging his 36-ounce war club for the Braves in Boston.

Tales of the antics of Germany Schaefer abound, but perhaps the best is the story about a homer he hit back in 1906. In June of that year Schaefer and his Tiger teammates visited Chicago for a series against the White Sox. In the final game of the series Schaefer rode the bench while Doc White and Red Donahue locked up in a pitcher's duel. The Sox were up, 2-1, in the top of the ninth when, with two outs and Charley O'Leary on base, Tiger manager Bill Armour sent Schaefer in to pinch-hit for Donahue. Germany strode to the plate and proclaimed to all within earshot: "Ladies and gentlemen, permit me to introduce to you Herman Schaefer, premier batsman of the world. He will now step to the plate and demonstrate to you his marvelous skill!" At that, Germany proceeded to knock a Doc White fastball out of the park, putting the Tigers up by a run. Hustling to first, the Dutchman slid into the bag, jumped up, dusted himself off, doffed his cap and exclaimed: "At the quarter, Schaefer leads by a length!" He turned for second and repeated the act, this time declaring: "At the half, Schaefer leads by two lengths!" Third base: "At three-quarters, Schaefer leads by a mile." And finally, following a tremendous slide at home, Schaefer announced: "Ladies and gentlemen, this concludes this afternoon's performance." The Sox were shut down in their half of the ninth and the Tigers headed home with the victory.

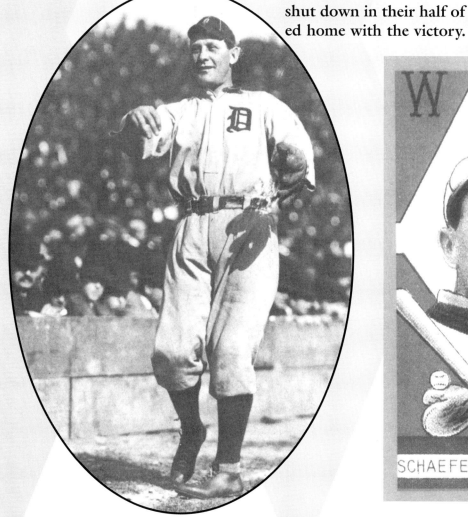

SCHAEFER WASHINGTON AM.

While Germany Schaefer was the first great baseball clown, Nick Altrock was the first to make a living at it. It should be noted, however, that Altrock started off as a top-notch pitcher, not a prankster. In a three-year stretch starting in 1904, Nick won 62 games for the White Sox and, in 1906, helped lead the "Hitless Wonders" to the World's Championship. But success didn't last long, and Nick soon found himself floundering in the minors. When he finally returned to the majors in 1912 it was as a coach and clown for Clark Griffith's Washington Nationals. The Old Fox teamed Altrock with the great Schaefer and attendance jumped wherever Washington played.

When Schaefer left for the Federal League in 1915, Altrock went solo. Acts in which he juggled, walked a "tight-rope" on the base lines (he stole that one from Schaefer's repertoire), and imitated umpires were crowd pleasers–but the buffoonery all began with his famous shadow-boxing shtick. According to Altrock, the famed routine started one day when the Nats couldn't buy a hit off Cleveland southpaw Vean Gregg:

"I was sitting beside Clark Griffith on the bench and, in those days, there were more pleasant places to sit than beside Clark Griffith when his team was being beaten. I was just wondering if I should ask for my release and get a job trucking dynamite over mountain roads or tell John Ringling I would like

to train some of his ferocious lions when Griff turned to me and said: 'You big jinx, I wonder what I hired you for.'

"Of course, I could have told him I was hired as a coach and not as a mascot but I did not think of that until the next day. The real things I wanted to say I had to keep to myself or take the next train out of town. But, I had to say something so I told him if I had a chance on the coaching lines I could break up the game.

"'I don't care what you do,' said Griff, 'as long as you take that handsome face of yours away from me.'

"So I went to the third base coaching lines. Half way on what I was figuring the longest journey in my life, I happened to recall that, the night before, I had seen a motion picture of Johnny Kilbane, then the featherweight boxing champion, doing some shadow boxing and decided to put on a burlesque of that act. It went over big. The fans ate it up. So did the players, including Vean Gregg. Being a left hander, like myself, he forgot all about the game and eased up in his pitching. We scored four runs that inning and eventually won the game."

Below, Altrock clowns with (who else?) a half-dozen other clowns at Griffith Stadium, June 25, 1921.

A dozen years after pairing Altrock and Schaefer, Clark Griffith, in a case of "déja vu all over again" (thanks Yogi), plucked yet another former major league pitcher from the minors to coach. Al Schacht was never the pitcher that Altrock had been, but he was every bit the clown. Though they first paired in the early '20s when Schacht was pitching for the Senators, the reunited duo now concentrated heavily on their comedy act. Altrock and Schacht teamed together for over a decade, clowning during the season, at the World Series, in off-season vaudeville tours, or any-where they could get booked. By the late '20s the partners had a falling out and rarely spoke to one another, but the act continued. Finally, in 1935, Schacht joined the Red Sox coaching staff, and a few years later he quit coaching altogether to take his act on the road. Schacht continued as "The Clown Prince of Baseball" until he was in his eighties.

Clockwise from top left: Altrock and Schacht lead a band onto the field at Griffith Stadium prior to the opening game of the 1924 World Series; Schacht and his giant glove prepare to stop anything, from a knuckleball to a freight train; a promotional cartoon of the Altrock and Schacht duo; the comedians roll the infield while the fans roll in the aisles, 1928; Schacht mimics the tosses of Boston third baseman Pinky Higgins at the '46 World Series in Fenway Park.

Bill Veeck once called Jackie Price "the greatest baseball entertainer in the country." That's quite a compliment coming from a guy who knew a thing or two about pleasing a crowd. In fact, Veeck found Price so enticing a draw that in August of 1946, the Indians' owner purchased Price from the Oakland Oaks and placed him on Cleveland's major league roster. Price managed to get in to a handful of big league games, but it was the miraculous feats he performed before the ballgame that paid his bills. Price's stunts were at once astounding, bizarre, and hilarious. He could catch balls in his pants, in his shirt, or while standing on

his head. His ability to remain suspended upside-down from his ankles for over fifteen minutes while taking batting practice was nothing short of miraculous. Just how he managed to hit two balls with one swing of the bat–sending one forward and the other behind him–was stupefying. He could simultaneously throw three balls to three different players or, from home plate, throw two balls at once: one to a pitcher on the mound and the other to an infielder on second. In his best known act, Jackie would drive his jeep around the outfield, tracking down and catching fungoes hit from home.

Max Patkin continued the clowning tradition forged by Schaefer, Altrock, and Schacht, inheriting the treasured title of "Clown Prince of Baseball." Equipped with a uniform a dozen sizes too big, and gifted with a rubber face, rubber legs, and a schnozz so large that it could have dropped the rest of his body and gone solo, Patkin spent more than fifty years cracking up crowds in practically every ballpark in the country. Fans and ballplayers alike never ceased to be astounded and amused by Max's alarming ability to transform himself into a human geyser, spontaneously spouting a shower of water high above his pursed lips.

Patkin through the ages. Clockwise from far left: 1930, 1977, 1959, 1963. Here, Max handles the lumber, 1963.

He Lightly Doffed his Hat ..

Ernest Thayer, above left, penned "Casey at the Bat" in 1888. Little did the former Harvard Lampoon editor know that his verse would become one of the best loved poems in American history. Thayer's ballad was a brilliant mixture of comedy, tragedy, and the inevitable failures that shape our national pastime. But credit for "Casey"'s popularity must go not only to its father, but also to the man who raised the child actor, singer, comedian DeWolf Hopper. Hopper was no stranger to baseball for he had long been a baseball fan and often took part in games between clubs comprised of Broadway actors (facing page, bottom). It was Hopper's countless recitations of the poem that established "Casey" as a part of the American vernacular. The link between "Casey" and Hopper became so close that it was once suggested that the actor change the final stanza to read:

> *OH, SOMEWHERE IN THE FAVORED LAND THE SUN IS SHINING BRIGHT;*
> *THE BAND IS PLAYING SOMEWHERE AND SOMEWHERE HEARTS ARE LIGHT;*
> *AND SOMEWHERE MEN ARE LAUGHING, AND SOMEWHERE CHILDREN SHOUT;*
> *BUT WHATEVER ELSE IS HAPPENING, HOPPER'LL BE STRIKING CASEY OUT.*

It's lucky that Thayer didn't have Casey batting in a game from 1887. It was in that season that it took four, not three, strikes for the batter to strike out. Casey would still have one coming and if he had struck out on four, the poem would no doubt have faded into obscurity.

The popularity of "Casey" has long withstood the test of time. Directly below is a page from a 1912 illustrated book, one of hundreds (if not thousands) of printings of the poem. Wallace Beery steps up to the plate, as he plays the title role in a 1927 film version of "Casey at the Bat."

These fellows weren't shy about displaying the championship banner for their victorious 'Keystone' team, representing International Harvester. Industrial and trade leagues were popular forms of lower-level organized baseball during the first few decades of the 20th century. It seems every factory and corporation of the era had a baseball club: Cumberland Telephone Company, Lincoln Cleaning and Dye Works, Toledo Railway and Light Company, National Malleable Casting Company, Ferro Machine & Foundry, Mechanical Rubber Company, and, from Medical Lake, Washington, the Eastern Hospital for the Insane Base Ball Club. Whether the nine was comprised of employees or patients is a mystery.

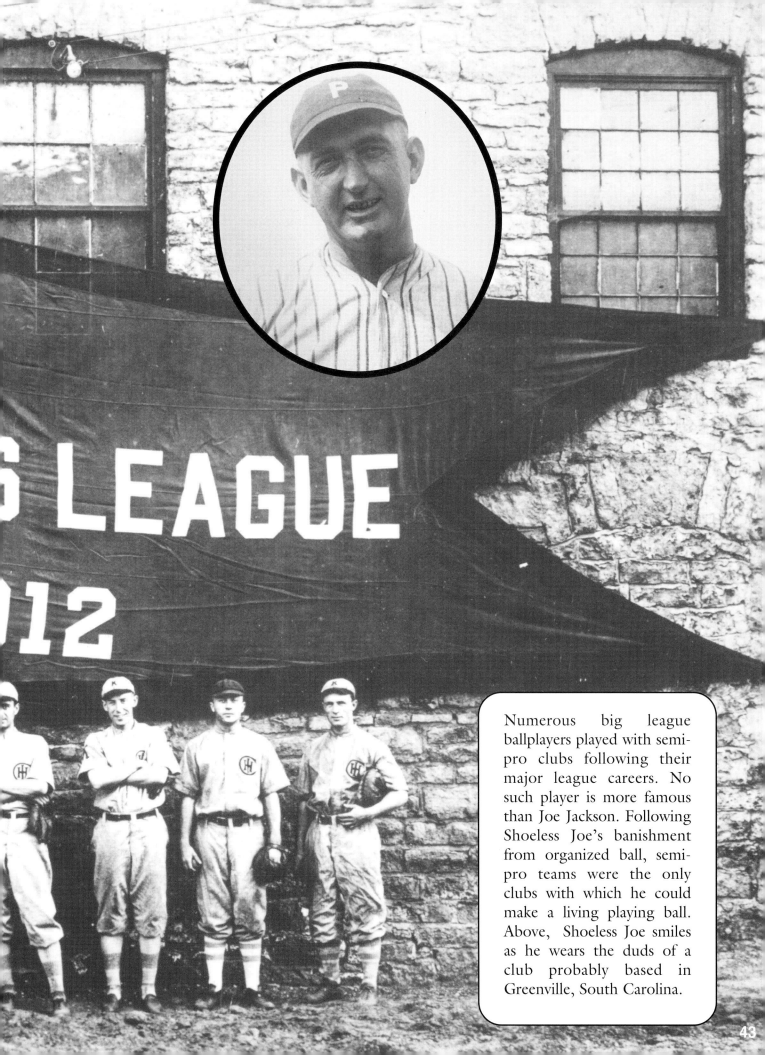

Numerous big league ballplayers played with semi-pro clubs following their major league careers. No such player is more famous than Joe Jackson. Following Shoeless Joe's banishment from organized ball, semi-pro teams were the only clubs with which he could make a living playing ball. Above, Shoeless Joe smiles as he wears the duds of a club probably based in Greenville, South Carolina.

Ever since the 1860 Brooklyn Excelsiors embarked on the first great baseball tour (that of New York State), barnstorming ball clubs have been a top gate attraction, especially in small town U.S.A.

Originally the House of David team played only at the religious sect's headquarters in Benton Harbor, Michigan. Eventually, however, the team grew so popular and the opportunity to proselytize became so inviting, that the club hit the road. Posters and broadsides such as those seen above and right advertised local games played by the bewhiskered ballplayers.

In 1934, Satchel Paige, on loan from the Pittsburgh Crawfords, helped the HoD club breeze through the prestigious Denver *Post* baseball tournament. Satch won 3 games, pitched 28 innings and struck out 44, as the "bearded beauties" finished the tournament with a record of 7-0.

Numerous well-known ballplayers joined up with the HoD club, though not all of them donned beards. Jackie Mitchell, famed for her back-to-back whiffs of Babe Ruth and Lou Gehrig in a 1931 exhibition game, pitched with the HoD club for over four years. Jackie's contract called for $1,000 a month! Babe Didrikson, picking up a similar stipend, pitched hundreds of times for the HoD barnstormers. Other major leaguers who at one time or another played with the HoD include Larry Jansen, Sig Jakucki, and Frank McCormick.

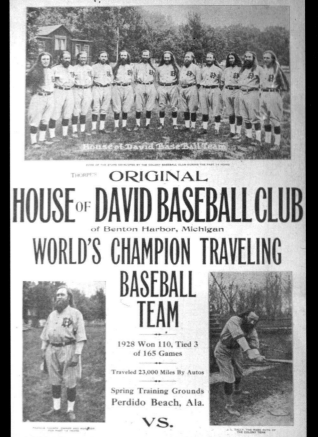

HOUSE OF DAVID" PITCHING

WHEN PITCHER MOONEY MOUNTS THE HILL
    WITH HAIR AND WHISKERS FLOWING,
THE STUFF HE'LL PUT UPON THE PILL
    WILL HAVE THE BATTERS GOING.
THEY WILL NOT EVEN MAKE A FOUL
    OR HAMMER OUT A FAIR BALL;
AND THEY WILL MAKE AN AWFUL HOWL
    WHEN MOONEY HURLS THE HAIR BALL.
        – Author unknown.

In 1931, 44-year-old Pete Alexander signed a $1,000 per month contract to manage and pitch for the House of David club. Alexander's contract stipulated that he pitch at least two innings every game (a requirement that he fulfilled more than 170 times that season!) and that he receive 25¢ a day for a shave. Unlike the rest of his club, Pete played sans whiskers. At left, Ol' Pete talks it over with his charges. At one time, shortstop Dutch Faust (far right) was offered a major league contract, but his refusal to shave nixed the deal.

Another star for the HoD, a pitcher named Mooney, was at one time offered a contract to take the mound for the Cubs. He chose instead to stay with the HoD. Efforts to identify Mooney in the photo at right have proven fruitless, though it's likely that he is the one with the long hair and beard.

Many barnstorming clubs used crazy gimmicks to attract a crowd. The House of David club wore beards, various Bloomer Girl clubs fielded all-female nines, and the Indianapolis Clowns perfected the fine art of baseball clowning. The Clowns featured the great baseball comic King Tut (aka Elmer King), and later, non-clowning female ballplayers Toni Stone (right) and Connie Morgan.

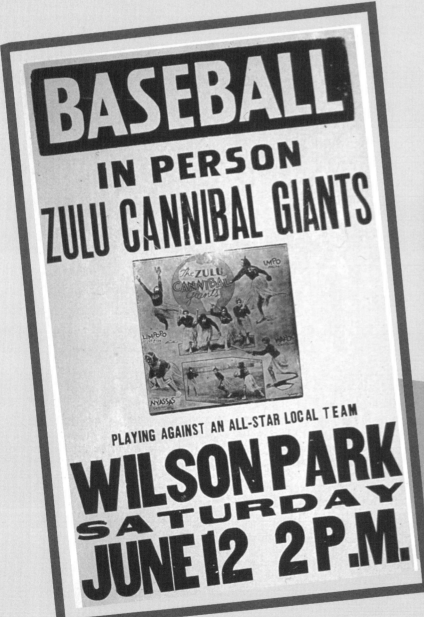

The Zulu Cannibal Giants (above) had one of the more outlandish acts on the barnstorming circuit. Billed as the "world's greatest novelty attraction," the club featured ballplayers clothed in grass skirts and adorned with colorful "war paint." This promotional poster advertises a game to be played at Wilson Park in Nashville, Tennessee, in June of '54.

The wit, wisdom, and philosophical genius of the legendary Satchel Paige is one of baseball's greatest treasures. Bill Veeck called Paige "a skinny Paul Bunyon, born to be everybody's most memorable character." Indeed, Satch's character was topped only by his pitching ability. When Veeck hired Paige to pitch for the '48 Indians, the joke was on those who thought the signing was just another one of Veeck's publicity stunts. Despite his advanced age (a matter of conjecture anyway), Satch posted a stellar 2.48 ERA and 6-1 record to help Cleveland to the pennant. As Satch once said: "Age is a question of mind over matter. If you don't mind, it don't matter."

Right is a Kansas City Monarchs souvenir adorned with Satch's likeness.

Below Satch visits with Dizzy Dean. Ol' Diz is perhaps the only other ballplayer of the era (though Satch spanned quite a few eras, didn't he?) with a character to rival that of Paige.

Ballclubs comprised of Native Americans were not uncommon during the heyday of barnstorming teams. John Olson's Cherokee Indian Base Ball Club toured throughout the country and at one time featured famed female pitcher (and future wife of Olson) Maud Nelson. And Jim Thorpe was the draw on an Indian ball team that traveled during the mid-1920s. The most famous Indian baseball club was that organized in 1897 by Guy Green. Green's Nebraska Indians (below and to the right,

with Guy Green in the top photo, standing at far right) toured through the Midwest to small towns like Jewell Junction, Iowa, Apple River, Illinois, Fort Recovery, Ohio, and Coldwater, Michigan. While the majority of players were indeed American Indians, a few "palefaces" were employed to fill out the roster.

Below, in front of a hodge-podge of buildings and teepees in turn-of-the-century Wisconsin, a baseball game is in progress. Note the batter taking a healthy cut and the various players scurrying for position. No doubt this field gave some pretty tough hops, but who says that you need a well-groomed ballfield to play baseball for the fun of it?

This color postcard advertises Guy Green's Nebraska Indians. Boasting that they were the "only ones on Earth," the popularity of the club was augmented by a sporadically published booklet entitled *Fun and Frolic with an Indian Ball Team*. The fellows at left and right are dressed in full Indian costume, but what's the story of the clown in the middle? Let Guy Green tell it himself:

"In the larger towns I often advertise my games by a ballyho stunt. Tobey (a white ballplayer with the club) puts on a clown costume which I carry with me, and in company with the Indians in savage dress, announces the games upon the streets. One season we had been playing the smaller towns of central Illinois for several weeks and opportunity for a good ballyhoo had been sadly lacking. The clown suit was moldering away in the trunk and becoming lonesome from disuse. We were booked for a game in Illiopolis, and were anxious to win it in such an impressive way that the victory would never be forgotten, because Illiopolis, which had only a little country team, had previously beaten us by close scores. Tobey was seized by a bright idea which we proceeded to put into execution. We secured a disreputable old tramp suit, a pair of shoes which gapped in a dozen places and a grip which would have disgraced a suburban ashpile. Tobey carefully packed his clown suit in his grip, donned his tramp attire, and by the consent of the conductor of our train, rode into Illiopolis on the blind baggage. He dropped off the cars and went up town by way of back alleys and unfrequented streets. The rest of us repaired to our hotel. Shortly after, I was in consultation with the Illiopolis manager, who was the leading druggist of the town, when a tough looking specimen of the genus hobo, carrying a battered old satchel, shuffled into the store, deposited his cigarette butt carefully on the counter and asked for the local ball man. Having secured his ear, Tobey unfolded a tale of woe a mile long. He told how he had been travelling as a clown with a little circus which

had recently stranded on the other side of Decatur, how he was a ball player and a good pitcher, and would like a chance to work against the Nebraska Indians. The Illiopolis man questioned him closely and then turned him down, saying he did not want to monkey with any tramps. Then Tobey turned to me, and with tears choking his voice, asked if there was any chance to get on with me, and ended by begging for something to eat. I gave him a quarter and told him to eat at a restaurant but not to come fooling around our hotel. Then I asked him if he had a ball suit, but he said he had nothing left but his clown clothes which he had brought with him from the circus. He proudly said, however, that he owned a pair of ball shoes. Finally I told him to put on such costume as he happened to have and come out to the grounds in the afternoon. Then he limped disconsolately away, bought him a meal in a cheap restaurant and with the aid of some small boys found a barn in which to dress.

"Before the hour for the game arrived, everyone in town knew of the tramp ball player who was in the village, and when Tobey came onto the grounds a little late, dressed in his clown suit, every farmer present pointed his finger at him and said, 'That's the feller that travelled with the busted show, and claims to be a ball player. I hope the Injun manager lets him pitch this afternoon, and we'll show 'im what our boys can do to 'im.' None of my players would have anything to do with Tobey, and he was compelled to warm up with a high school lad who borrowed a big mitt from one of the Illiopolis players. The game finally started and Tobey went into the box for me. For five innings he shut out the Illiopolis team. Then he shed his clown blouse, exposed the Indian shirt which he was wearing underneath it, rid himself of his clown hat and put on his Indian cap and the secret was out. A roar went up from the spectators when they realized the clever ruse that had been worked. We won the game eleven to two."

Three of our Star Players.   Established 1897. Only Ones on Earth.
Green's Nebraska Indian Baseball Team.
Guy W. Green, Lincoln, Nebraska. Sole Owner and Manager.

Spoofing the plight of the catcher and the dangers of the ballfield, these multicolored trade cards were popular forms of advertising in the 1880s. Except in the case of the *Sporting Life* cards, these were initially printed without advertising text and only after a set was purchased would the advertisements be added to the appropriate blank spaces.

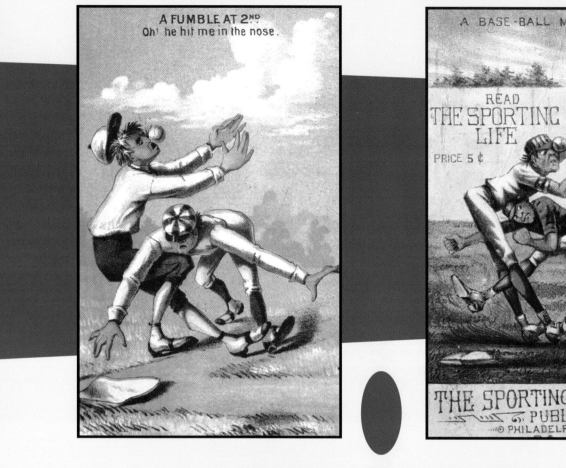

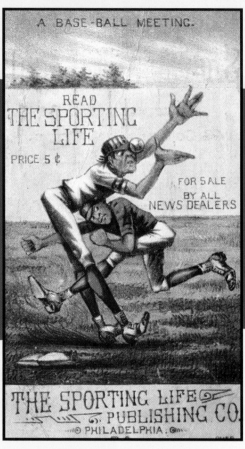

The card (top left, facing page) advertising the Royal Show Company, parodies "Baby" Anson. In 1871, Anson was one of the youngest players in the newly formed National Association. His age and his penchant for whining on the ballfield resulted in one of the first nicknames ever bestowed on a ballplayer. Another card (above) shows Jack Glasscock, shortstop for the Indianapolis Hoosiers from 1887-89, taking one in the eye. Just makes you want to go out and buy some new clothes from Max Stadler & Company, don't it?

CALL FOR THE
ROYAL SHOE,
Men's, Boys' and Youth's.

Oh, Mamma! BABY ANSON.

STEVENSON & CO.
GENUINE REDUCTION IN SUMMER CLOTHING
Straw Hats, Underwear, Flannel Shirts, &c.
STEVENSON & CO.

A WILD THROW

A CATCHER AT THE END OF THE SEASON.

READ THE
SPORTING LIFE
5 cts.

FOR SALE BY ALL
NEWS-DEALERS

Compliments of
THE SPORTING LIFE PUBLISHING CO
PHILADELPHIA, PA. U.S.

BASE BALL

GETS THERE JUST THE SAME
The catcher of the visiting team is a little bow-
legged, but suffers no inconvenience on that ac-
count by reason of the above ingenious device.

FROM "TEXAS SIFTINGS"
BY PERMISSION.

TIP TOP WEEKLY

"An ideal publication for the American Youth"

Issued weekly—By Subscription, $2.50 per year. Entered as Second Class Matter at the N. Y. Post Office by STREET & SMITH

No. 228,   Price, Five Cents.

FRANK MERRIWELL'S SPEED OR BREAKING THE CHICAGO COLTS

BY BURT L. STANDISH

RUNNING IN THE SAME DIRECTION AS THE BALL, THE CENTER-FIELDER, WITH OUTSTRETCHED HANDS, CAUGHT IT

For decades, the children of America were entertained weekly by heroic exploits on the western plains, in the secret recesses of the inner city, and, yes, on the ball field! Frank Merriwell, and his kid brother Dick, performed miraculous feats of athleticism while their competitors labored under other titles like Frank Manley of *Young Athlete's Weekly* and Fred Fearnot of *Work and Win*. Each and all were as exuberant and optimistic as the hopeful youths that read of their adventures.

Baseball, more than any other sport, lends itself to the written word, whether it be fact or fiction. Indeed, reading baseball was, and still is, a national pastime in its own right. Whether it's the bush league, the hot stove league, or the intergalactic league, baseball fans have always had an insatiable thirst for books about the game they love.

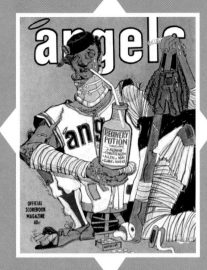

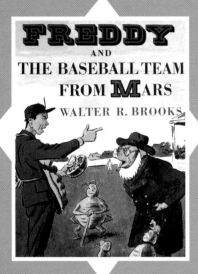

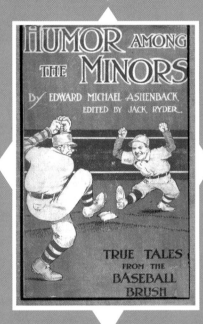

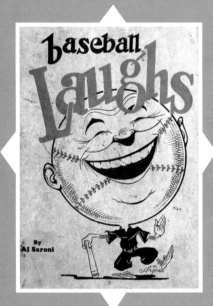

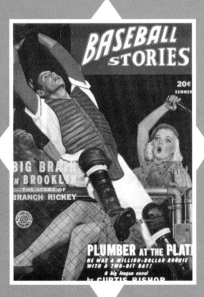

Four professional teams in Cuba dominated the island's Golden Age, the 1940s and 1950s. These colorful logos adorned all kinds of Cuban fan paraphernalia, representing, clockwise from upper left: Cienfuegos (Elephants), Marianao (Tigers), Habana (Lions), and Almandares (Scorpions). At center is Martin Dihigo, generally acknowledged as the greatest Cuban player of all time. A crushing competitor as a pitcher or a hitter, Dihigo starred in the U.S. Negro Leagues, and is a Hall of Famer in more countries than any other player. His placques reside in Cuba, Mexico, Venezuela, and the United States.

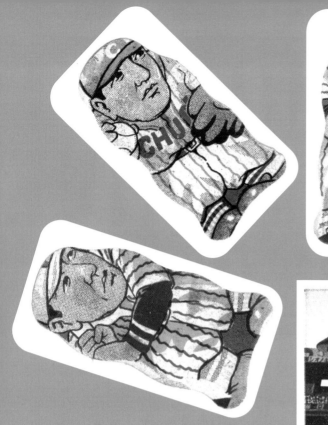

真田投手

Baseball cards have been around since the 1860s, and baseball itself was introduced to Japan just a decade later. So it's no surprise that, just as in the States, trading cards featuring the top players of the game were (and are) popular collectibles for the baseball hungry youth of Japan.

Above are five diecut menko from the 1940s. The ballplayers depicted are, left to right, Shigeharu Morishita, Kiyoshi Sugiura, Tetsuharu Kawakami, "Bozo" Wakabayashi, and Takao Misono.

A Hall-of-Fame first baseman, Kawakami was known as "The Lou Gehrig of Japan." He played from 1938 to '58 and was a five-time batting champion. Wakabayashi, another Hall-of-Famer, was born and raised in Hawaii. After starring as both a football and baseball player in the late 1920s in Honolulu, "Bozo" left for Japan where he pitched for sixteen seasons–twice posting single season ERAs under 1.10! His final career won-loss record was 237-144 with an ERA of 1.99.

The color bromide card at center shows Hall-of-Fame pitcher Juzo Sanada. In 1950, Sanada was 39-12 for the Shochiku Robins, accounting for nearly 40 percent of the club's 98 victories that season. Only three other pitchers have ever won more games in a single season in Japan.

The rectangular menko at left is of Atsushi Aramaki with the Mainichi Orions. Known as the "Japanese Bob Feller," Aramaki was a fireballing pitcher who won Rookie of the Year honors in 1950. That year he was 26-8 with a 2.06 ERA, and helped pace the Orions to the Japanese Series Championship. Aramaki finished his thirteen year career with a won-loss record of 173-107 and entered the Hall of Fame in 1985.

WESTERN BLOOMER GIRL
BASE BALL CLUB

BLOOMER GIRLS VS. LOCAL CLUB

CLEAN MORAL AND REFINED

= MAUD NELSON =
CHAMPION LADY PITCHER OF THE WORLD

Maud Nelson was a star pitcher and influential club owner on the barnstorming circuit for more than thirty-five years. Her first professional gig came as a 16-year-old pitcher with the Boston Bloomer Girls in 1897. By the time she was 30, Nelson owned, managed, and pitched for the Western Bloomer Girls, the most successful all-female club of the era. Well, almost all-female . . . Bloomer Girl clubs often played with a handful of men in the lineup. Back in 1912, a teenaged Rogers Hornsby, dressed in drag, once played ball with the Boston Bloomer Girls!

MACK SENNETT COMEDIES

Mack Sennett gave the movies the Keystone Kops and pie-in-the-face slapstick, but with his Bathing Beauties, Sennett pushed the limits (such as they were) of featuring scantily clad women on the silver screen. No matter what the plot, Sennett somehow managed to work the Bathing Beauties in to his movies. What better way to bolster moviehouse ticket sales than to spotlight a baseball club comprised of shapely women in bathing suits, as above?

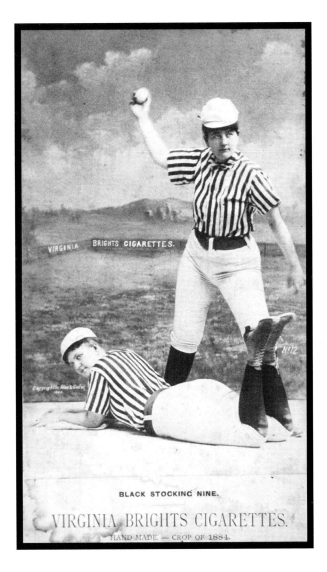

VIRGINIA BRIGHTS CIGARETTES.

BLACK STOCKING NINE.

VIRGINIA BRIGHTS CIGARETTES.
HAND-MADE — CROP OF 1884.

Women ballplayers were nothing new, of course, as the fair sex had been playing baseball since well before the turn of the century. The exaggerated pose and false background seen in the poster to the left was not uncommon for 1880s promotional premiums, whether they featured women or men.

Bill Veeck understood that the business of baseball and baseball for the fun of it were not mutually exclusive. The self-proclaimed "hustler" combined the two worlds of baseball far better (and more often) than any owner before or since–Veeck was the ultimate baseball innovator. In 1942, as owner of the American Association Milwaukee Brewers, Veeck devised a moveable right field fence. When a club with lefty sluggers came to town, the fence would go up. Otherwise, the fence would be out of the way and the short porch in right would remain as is. Eventually, Veeck tried out the inevitable: with the opposition at bat Veeck put the fence in place; with the Brewers at bat the fence was removed. The experiment lasted one game, after which Veeck was accorded baseball's ultimate compliment: the rules were changed to outlaw such practices.

"Mr. Ideas," as Veeck was sometimes called, gave us Wrigley Field's ivy covered walls, Comiskey Park's exploding scoreboard, and the outrageous Bermuda shorts worn by the 1976 White Sox. He orchestrated Disco Demolition Night and Grandstand Managers Day; the former ending up in a forfeit loss for his '79 Sox, with the latter producing a rare win for his '51 Browns. Near the end of that wacky '51 season, "Sport Shirt Bill" concocted a plan to sign Buddy Blattner from the Phillies reserve list, strap a two-way radio to his back, and have him broadcast a Browns game while playing third base! Too bad it never happened.

Below is Bill with his kids. At far right is son Mike, who is currently carrying on the Veeck tradition with the Northern League's St. Paul Saints.

And, of course, there was Eddie Gaedel. In the photo below, Matt Batts is at left, Jim McDonald is at right, and, in case you're wondering, that's Gaedel in the middle. In Game 2 of the August 19, 1951, Browns-Athletics doubleheader, the 43-inch high Gaedel walked in his legendary pinch hitting appearance. However, few remember that Eddie actually popped out in his first appearance that day! Explanation: Between games of the doubleheader, Veeck staged a celebration honoring the fiftieth anniversary of both the American League and Falstaff Brewery, the Brown's radio sponsor. (Actually, nobody seemed to know exactly when Falstaff was founded, but that didn't stop Veeck from throwing a party.) The festivities culminated with the arrival a giant birthday cake at home plate and the subsequent introduction of a "genuine Brownie." At that, Eddie popped out (of the cake) and into baseball history.

For more information on the talented Mr. McKeown, we refer you to the following publications: "Unicycling For the Fun of It," "Shaving For the Fun of It," "Pocket Billiards For the Fun of It," and "Bicycle Trick Riding For the Fun of It."

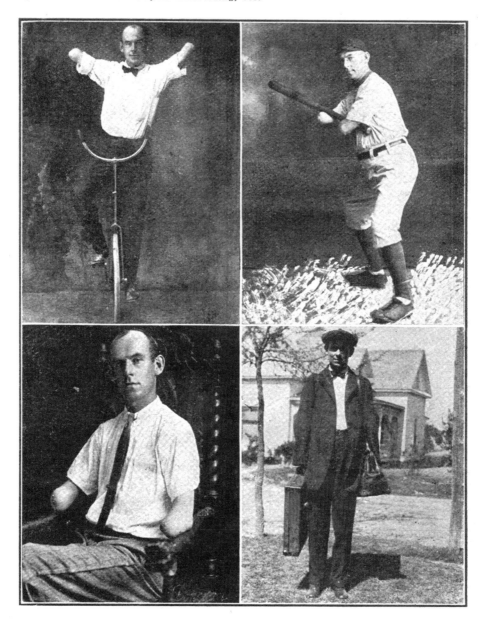

THESE PICTURES SHOW

FRANK McKEOWN

THE ARMLESS BALL PLAYER

OF PASSAIC, N. J.

Who when 13 years of age, lost both his arms in a rubber factory. Since that time he has learned to use carpenter tools, shave with a straight razor, play ball, bowl, pocket billiards and bicycle trick riding, etc.

"I am not one of the ball players with baseball brains. No, indeed. In fact, some people have told me that I was lacking in brains of any kind. The statement has been repeated so many times that at times I have nursed a suspicion that perhaps it might be true. But I will hardly go that length. In fact I believe that I do have a little sense. I have sense enough at any rate to realize how dumb some of us players are and that proves that I know something." –Casey Stengel

"I've lived a long, hard life and I've done everything. I don't remember it all, but when somebody tells me they seen me do something out there on the ball field, I tell them they are right. I must of done it. That's how it is when you live a long, hard life."

In December of 1950, the White Sox and Red Sox completed a major trade. Looking for the Ol' Professor's opinion, a reporter explained the trade: "The Red Sox get Ray Scarborough and Bill Wight from the White Sox for Al Zarilla, Joe Dobson, and Dick Littlefield. What do you think?" Stengel reflected for a moment and then replied: "Well, the feller ought to help them."

Some say that Casey was one of the greatest managers of all time, while others argue that with the ballplayers the Yankees had, anyone could have won the pennant. Whoever is right, no one can deny that Casey was one of the greatest *non*-managers in the history of the game. Following the 1936 season, the Brooklyn brass fired manager Stengel, but as Casey still had a year left on his contract, the Dodgers had to pay Casey $15,000 for the '37 season. Not only was this $2,000 more than Casey had received in '36 (his contract was on a sliding scale), but it was significantly more than the salary of the man that would actually manage the Dodgers for '37, Burleigh Grimes!

Casey went to Brooklyn and looked over the club he was not to manage: "The more I know about the ball club, the better equipped I will be not to manage it. The Brooklyn club is not paying me not to watch them. They are just paying me not to manage them. I can not-watch a ball team with the best, but so long as I am not being paid not to watch."

Later, Casey reflected upon his experience as a non-manager: "There ain't a trick about non-managing that I don't know. I can non-coach from either first or third base, I can non-give a bunt or take sign with the best, and I can non-fine a bad-acting ball player anywheres from $50 to $1,000. No doubt many a fella has cleaned up in this field, non-managing here and non-managing there and pyramiding his fees into a nice little nest-egg. No doubt many a non-manager has retired with millions. But if I was giving advice to the growing boy, I would tell him to keep away from not managing, even though it netted me $15,000 a year. I would tell him, 'Don't be president, if you want to, or don't be a prize fighter, but don't don't manage.'"

NATIONAL BAS

APRIL 7-14.

SPORTING GOODS   FISHIN

For the true baseball fanatic, every week is "National Base Ball Week." But back in the '20s and '30s, one week each spring was so designated to promote baseball among the nation's youth. For the 1930 event, National League president John Heydler proclaimed: "The promotion of National Base Ball Week is an important an helpful work in American life. Nothing could be more beneficial to boys than to stimulate their interest in the National Game. Once you get a boy to play baseball, he will play every chance he gets until he reaches middle age. And the game develops him, mind and body. It gives him poise and speed and skill. It tests his character and develops his resourcefulness and teaches him patience." And, Mr. Heydler seems to have forgotten to mention, it makes him a faithful paying customer at the local ballpark. It's no coincidence that, in conjunction with the week long celebration, the *Sporting Goods Dealer*, a trade publication based in St. Louis, offered trophies and cash prizes to retail stores with the best display of baseball merchan-

dise and equipment. Certainly the establishments seen above were top candidates for first prize. (By the way, that's Wallace Beery as "Casey at the Bat" in the middle of the window, above right.)

Doubt that Abner Doubleday is the true father of baseball? Well, in 1941 the 87-year old fellow at right, the Reverend Charles Fayette Swift, recounted for the sporting press the days of his youth in Cooperstown, New York, when he batted against Doubleday himself! It was in 1865, a quarter of a century after the general first developed the game, that the young Swift faced the underhand pitches of the famed Civil War veteran. According to the newspapermen covering his story, Swift was one of two men alive who learned the game from Doubleday himself. Alas, no mention is made of the other lucky fellow. Yes, it's clearly stated on the "Scroll of Fame" (below) in Cooperstown: Major General Abner Doubleday invented our national pastime. Now, you're not going to doubt an ordained Methodist minister, the good folks from the news media, and the Baseball Hall of Fame, are you?

NATIONAL BASEBALL MUSEUM

IMMORTALS

TYRUS RAYMOND COBB
GEORGE HERMAN RUTH
JOHN HENRY WAGNER
CHRISTOPHER MATHEWSON
WALTER P. JOHNSON
NAPOLEON LAJOIE
DENTON TECUMSEH YOUNG
TRISTRAM E. SPEAKER
GROVER CLEVELAND ALEXANDER
GEORGE WRIGHT
MORGAN G. BULKELEY
BYRON BANCROFT JOHNSON
JOHN J. McGRAW
CONNIE MACK

THIS BUILDING HAS BEEN
ERECTED WITH THE OFFICIAL SANCTION
OF ORGANIZED BASEBALL AS A PERMAN-
ENT SHRINE OF THE NATIONAL GAME
AND AS A MEMORIAL TO ITS INVENTOR
MAJOR GENERAL ABNER DOUBLEDAY.

IN THE HALL OF FAME
THE IMMORTALS OF BASEBALL ARE RE-
PRESENTED BY BRONZE PLAQUES WHICH
HAVE BEEN PRESENTED TO THE NATIONAL
BASEBALL MUSEUM BY THE MAJOR LEAGUES.
THE IMMORTALS OF THE
PIONEER ERA OF THE NATIONAL GAME HAVE
BEEN CHOSEN BY A SPECIAL COMMITTEE
APPOINTED BY THE MAJOR LEAGUES.
THE IMMORTALS WHO
HAVE BECOME FAMOUS SINCE 1900 HAVE
BEEN ELECTED IN A NATION-WIDE POLL
OF THE BASEBALL WRITERS ASSOCIA-
TION OF AMERICA. FUTURE ELECTIONS
TO THE HALL OF FAME WILL BE CONDUC-
TED EACH YEAR IN A SIMILAR MANNER.

IMMORTALS

Speaking of good stories, there must be a dozen beauties about Frenchy Bordagaray . . . and a decent number of them are true, too! There was the time that Frenchy, while with the Dodgers, was on second when a Cubs pitcher sent a pick-off throw to Billy Herman covering the bag. It looked as if Frenchy was standing right on top of the base, but when Herman applied the tag Bordagaray was called out. Brooklyn manager Casey Stengel rushed to the scene, arguing the call. How could Frenchy be out when his foot had been on the base? The ump walked away without saying a word and, surprisingly, so did Frenchy. When Stengel returned to the dugout he asked Bordagaray why he didn't join in the argument.

"Well, Casey. I guess I was out."

"Out? How could you be out? You was standing on the bag!"

"Yeah, I was, but it was this way. While I was waiting for the pitcher to throw the ball I got a little bored and was tapping my foot. He must have got me between taps."

Then there was the time that Frenchy lost his cool and spit at an umpire. Unfortunately, he hit his target. When notified of the hefty fine levied by the league, Bordagaray remarked: "Well, it was more than I expectorated."

A fully adorned Frenchy poses for the camera on opening day at the Polo Grounds, 1936. Stengel told Bordagaray to lose the whiskers, but the young Dodger was reluctant. Finally, Stengel proclaimed: "I'm going to tell every catcher in the league to throw at your mustache when you're on the bases." Frenchy shaved and the baseball world had to wait another thirty-five years before the Oakland A's brought facial hair back to big league ball.

The Gashouse Gang was a wild, brash, cocky, hustling, dirty (in both senses of the word) and superb cast of characters so colorful it seemed as though they sprang straight from the pen of Ring Lardner. But they were real, winning three National League pennants and two World's Championships in the first five years of the 1930s.

"The Wild Horse of the Osage," Pepper Martin, was a hawk-nosed, broad-shouldered, muscle-bound Oklahoman who made the 1931 World Series all his own. In the first five games of the series against Connie Mack's Athletics, the rookie Martin banged out seven singles, four doubles, one homer, and stole four bases. Though Philadelphia shut him down for the final games of the series, the Cardinals prevailed. Prior to game three, the first played at Shibe Park, Martin (already with five hits and three stolen bases under his belt) posed with a Philly policeman. Apparently the constable was the only fellow in town who could arrest Pepper's penchant for purloining bases and hold him from further assaulting the battery of the A's.

Though the success of the Gashousers waned during the latter half of the decade, the club's zany antics did not. Below, Pepper Martin leads a fishin' trip, and at left he leads the 1938 edition of Pepper Martin's Musical Mudcats (left to right: Frenchy Bordagaray, Bill McGee, Lefty Weiland, Ripper Collins, and Martin).

Jay Hanna Dean or Jerome Herman Dean (take your pick) was a self-centered, egotistical, carefree, laugh-a-minute, cotton-picking (no, really–Papa Dean and all the kids worked in the cotton fields) fireballer. But he warn't no braggart 'cause "it ain't braggin' if you can back it up." And Dizzy could. In the split photo at left Diz (right) consoles brother Paul after the latter Dean gave up seven hits in just 2-1/3 innings against Brooklyn on August 24, 1935. Luckily, the Cards managed to come back from a 5-0 deficit that day and beat the Dodgers, 10-7. Diz's pep-talk must have done the trick, for the next day "Me'n Paul" pitched a pair of complete game victories as the Cards swept a doubleheader from the Dodgers at Ebbets Field.

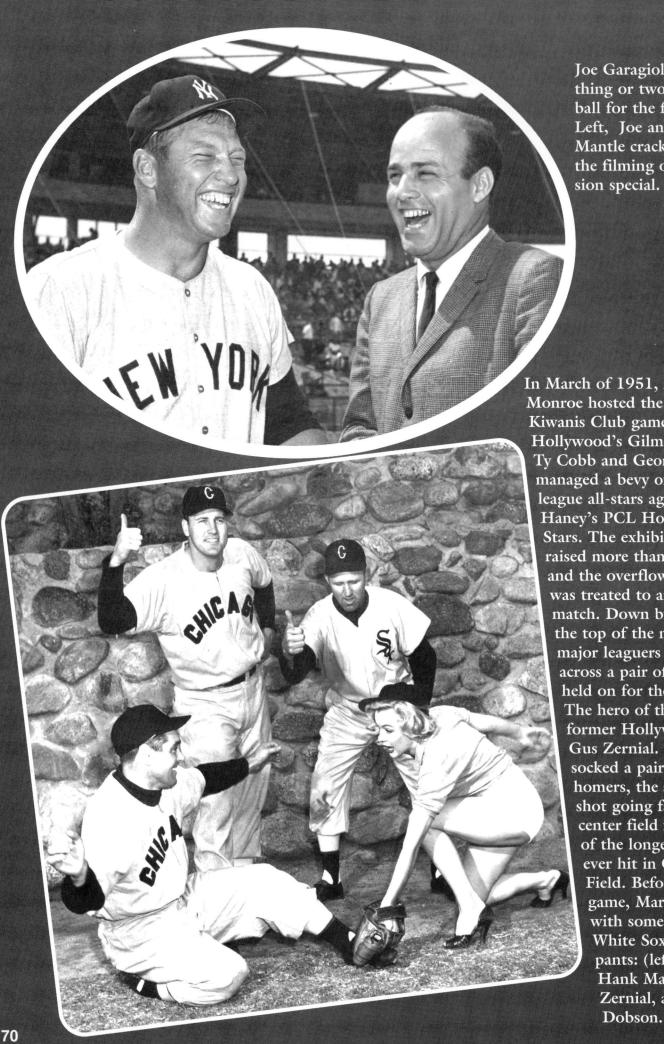

Joe Garagiola knows a thing or two about base ball for the fun of it. Left, Joe and Mickey Mantle crack up during the filming of a television special.

In March of 1951, Marilyn Monroe hosted the annual Kiwanis Club game at Hollywood's Gilmore Field. Ty Cobb and George Sisler managed a bevy of big league all-stars against Fred Haney's PCL Hollywood Stars. The exhibition game raised more than $20,000 and the overflow crowd was treated to an exciting match. Down by a run in the top of the ninth, the major leaguers pushed across a pair of runs and held on for the victory. The hero of the day was former Hollywood Star, Gus Zernial. Gus socked a pair of solo homers, the second shot going far over the center field fence, one of the longest blasts ever hit in Gilmore Field. Before the game, Marilyn posed with some of the White Sox participants: (left to right) Hank Majeski, Zernial, and Joe Dobson.

In 1950, American League batters absolutely shellacked the pitching of St. Louis Brown Harry Dorish. In spring training of '51 (below), Harry (now with the White Sox) wised up–if he was going to serve up balls the size of water- melons, he would wear a glove large enough to catch them.

On June 19, 1952, Brooklyn's Carl Erskine no-hit the visiting Cubs. Rain was falling in the third inning when Cubs pitcher Willie Ramsdell came to bat. Hoping to get through five innings so the game would count, Erskine pitched hurriedly. "I kept firing fast balls to Ramsdell and couldn't get one over." Ramsdell would prove to be the only Cub baserunner that day. A 44-minute rain-delay interrupted the game, but that didn't seem to bother Erskine: "When the game was interrupted, I went into the clubhouse and played bridge with Billy Cox, Duke Snider, and Ralph Branca. I bid four hearts–and I made it. Right then I knew it was my lucky day." Above, "Oisk" is mobbed by the Flatbush faithful after his near-perfect game.

Jimmy Piersall was twice an All-Star, twice a Gold-Glove outfielder, and twice as unpredictable as any other ballplayer of his era. When Piersall first began goofing around in the batter's box, on the bases, and in the outfield, it was a sign of his mental instability. Later, following his successful recovery from mental illness, he continued to clown around on the field. His antics were rarely disruptive and were usually just an attempt to entertain the fans who called him "Crazy Jim." In 1963, when Piersall hit his 100th career home run and ran backwards around the bases it was not a spur-of-the-moment joke. No, Jim had actually spent many an hour practicing backpedaling in anticipation of the event.

At left, it's Friday th 13 of April, 1962. Piersall (left) and Washington manager Mickey Vernon josh with pitcher Pete Burnside following a rain and snow short- ened game against Cleveland. Just six months earlier, Piersall had been traded from the Indians following a stellar season in which he won a Gol Glove and batted a career high .322, third best in the AL.

It's 1954 (above) and Johnny Antonelli couldn't be happier, as h chucks the cheek of teammate Dusty Rhodes for his game winning hi

The words of Casey Stengel, Satchel Paige, and Yogi Berra occupy an elite wing in the Hall of Fame of baseball quotes. Given the sheer volume of wacky, offbeat, and downright unintelligible statements that have been uttered by the threesome, one wonders how they ever found time to play ball. Indeed, it is probable that a good number of the words attributed to them were simply fabricated by the press. Here are some Yogi-isms that haven't yet made it into the vernacular:

"You've got to be careful if you don't know where you're going, because you might not get there."

"I'd rather be the Yankees' catcher than the president, and that makes me pretty lucky because I could never be the president."

"Slump? I ain't in no slump. I just ain't hitting."

"If you come to a fork in the road, take it."

"I want to thank you for making this day necessary."

"If people don't want to come out to the park, nobody's going to stop them."

"A nickel ain't worth a dime anymore."

"He must have made that (movie) before he died."

"You can observe a lot by watching."

"The other teams could make trouble for us if they win."

"I usually take a two-hour nap from one to four."

"We made too many wrong mistakes."

"If you can't imitate him, don't copy him."

"I got a touch of pantomime poisoning."

"Third ain't so bad if nothin' is hit to you."

"We're not exactly hitting the ball off the cover."

"In baseball, you don't know *nothing*."

Below, as Yogi handles the lumber: "So, I'm ugly. So what? I never saw anyone hit with his face."

Rules, rules, rules. The pitcher shall not bring his pitching hand in contact with his mouth or lips. The pitcher shall not apply a foreign substance of any kind to the ball. The pitcher shall not expectorate on the ball, either hand or his glove. The pitcher shall not rub the ball on his glove, person or clothing. The pitcher shall not deface the ball in any manner. The pitcher shall not deliver what is called the "shine" ball, "spit" ball, "mud" ball or "emery" ball.

Above, Gaylord Perry invites you to play "Where's Waldo" with the K-Y. On the sleeve? Under the cap? Over the shoulder? Off the chest? "I'd always have it in at least two places, in case the umpires would ask me to wipe off one. I never wanted to be caught out there-without anything. It wouldn't be professional."

Tug
McGraw, a screwball pitcher
(pun very much intended), always took
exception to being called a flake. He insisted
that he was a "Kellogg." Immediately following the
conclusion of the players strike of 1972, said Kellogg
went to Shea Stadium for practice. The first thing he did
was walk to the first base line, stand up straight and
place his cap over his heart. When asked what he was
doing, Tug replied: "I'm practicing the *Star-
Spangled Banner*. You know, after nine days
on strike, you forget the words."

Tommy Lasorda is a liar and a con! Ask anyone who ever played for the guy and they'll tell you so. Once, when managing Spokane, Tommy's club lost six games in a row. The skipper called a meeting and instead of chewing the team out, he calmly explained that losing streaks were a part of baseball. The fellows shouldn't fret. Why, the 1927 Yankees, the greatest team ever, once lost nine straight games! With that, Tommy's club went on a tear and ran away with the pennant. After the season ended, one of the Spokane players asked Lasorda if that great Yankee club really did lose nine in a row, to which Tommy replied: "How the hell should I know?" He pulled a similar stunt on Joe Ferguson when Walt Alston wanted the young outfielder to switch to catcher. Ferguson wasn't sure. Lasorda took Joe aside and rattled off the biggest names in catching history. Did Joe know that the great Mickey Cochrane started off as an outfielder? And Gabby Hartnett was a converted outfielder, too? And Ernie Lombardi? All were former outfielders, all became catchers, and all are in the Hall of Fame. Thus motivated, Ferguson made the switch to catcher. Never mind that the whole thing was a bunch of hooey. Yes, Lasorda's a liar and a con . . . and a Hall-of-Famer.

"Happy Birthday to Lou, Happy Birthday to Lou!" Left, Lou Brock celebrates his 38th birthday by feeding the Cards' Keith Hernandez some birthday cake. Someone must have told Lou "you can't have your cake and eat it, too."

Left, Bill Buckner gleefully displays his collection of jewelry. While the bracelets did well to charm Billy Buck's bat, perhaps he should have considered wearing them on his ailing ankles back in 1986.

More often than any other major leaguer in history, strikeout king Reggie Jackson, the self-proclaimed "straw that stirs the drink," was "the batter who whiffs the air." Left, Mr. October laughs as he gets a hold of nothing once again.

"Spaceman" Bill Lee (right) did little to dispel the stereotypes about southpaw pitchers. Rod Dedeaux, Lee's coach at Southern Cal, once said: "I always understood everything Casey Stengel said, which sometimes worried me. But I know that all my hours with Casey helped prepare me for Billy Lee."

Ebbets Field *was* baseball for the fun of it. It was Red and Vin. It was Hilda and her cowbell, Abe Stark and a free suit, and the Dodger Sym-Phony. It was yellow baseballs, a dropped third strike, and Reiser on a stretcher. It was Sisler's homer to left and Cookie's double to right. It was one bird under Casey's cap, two no-hitters by Vander Meer, three Dodgers on third, and four homers by Hodges. It was 297 feet to a crooked right field wall. It was Uncle Robby and Dazzy and Casey and Zack and Frenchy and Dixie and Dolph and Leo and Duke and Pee Wee and Campy and Gil and Jackie and Skoonj and Oisk and Newk and many, many more. And, alas, all too often it was a single to right, a host of Yankees running 'round the bases, a Dodger loss, and a cry of "Wait 'til next year." Here's Game 3 of the '49 Series and, with the bases loaded, Yankee Johnny Mize has just singled to right off Ralph Branca to break a 1-1 tie in the top of the ninth.

The highlight of the annual New York Baseball Writers' meeting at Bear Mountain, New York, was always the New York versus Brooklyn baseball game. The 1949 contest ended in favor of the New Yorkers, with Mel Allen pulling off some defensive dazzlers in the outfield and New York Times reporter Lou Effrat pitching tough against the Brooklynites. Facing page, top, Branch Rickey, cigar in mouth, takes a wide one. But, wait a second! Umpire Durocher is calling it a strike . . . and the ball hasn't even hit Burt Shotton's mitt! There's sure to be a rhubarb.

Since the scribes were playing the game, it was only fair that a player got to write up the contest. Here's what reporter (and sometime Dodger pitcher) Rex Barney penned:

"Having waited for years for this opportunity to be the man that bites the dog, it gives me great pleasure to report the manner in which the New York writers defeated the Brooklyn writers, 5 to 2, in their annual and alleged game.

"Herb Goren, a press box expert at Ebbets Field, who has been writing about my 'disgraceful, abominable and just plain lousy control' for the past few seasons, blew a 2 to 0 lead in the sixth inning, while walking across three runs. Goren, who should have been yanked during his wild streak, remained in the game, because, by a strange coincidence, he happened to be the manager, too."

On July 10, 1934, the tiny village of North Brookfield, Massachusetts, celebrated Connie Mack Day. Displaying his old catching form below, Mack was born in nearby East Brookfield, while longtime baseball fan George M. Cohan, wielding the ash, once lived in North Brookfield. Calling the balls and strikes is Frank Bird, a native of nearby Spencer, and a former cup-of-coffee Cardinal catcher (say *that* ten times fast) from 1892. Interestingly, North Brookfield was also home to a pair of former major league catchers: the brothers Bergen. Bill was an eleven year backstop with Cincinnati and Brooklyn, while Marty is best remembered for having tragically and brutally taken his life (as well as those of his wife and kids) back in 1900.

To the left, Jimmy Dykes, Al Simmons, and Mule Haas (L-R) get some kicks playing "Yankee Doodle" before a 1934 Comiskey Park contest. They certainly weren't having much fun on the field that year, as the cellar dwelling Chisox missed losing a hundred by only one game.

Charley horses, sore muscles, aching backs, lame arms. Get out the liniment! As Casey Stengel put it, Old-Timers games are like airplane landings . . . if you can walk away from them, they're successful.

On June 8, 1926, Wrigley Field in Los Angeles was the site of an Old-Timers benefit game with the profits going to help less-fortunate, aged ballplayers. More than fifty former semipro, California, and Pacific Coast Leaguers took part in the fun, including big name stars like Gavvy Cravath, Sam Crawford, Mike Donlin, and Pol Perritt. Red Grange tossed out the first ball to Gene Tunney, and auto racing legend Barney Oldfield was one of a number of celebrity umpires. Below, Jimmy Kerwin (standing at left) and Lew Nordyke (standing right) help wheel out Old Timers Johnny Beall (sitting left) and Mike Ready.

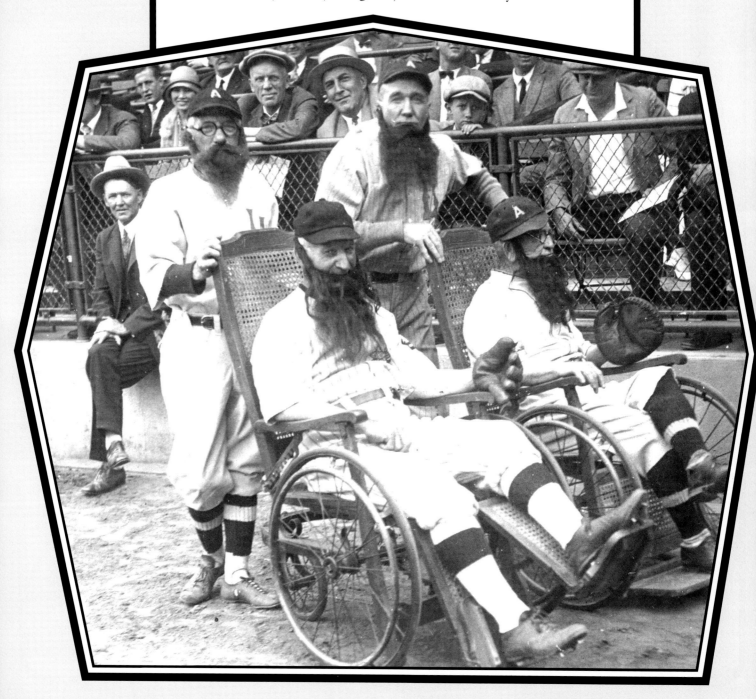

Below, a group of former Athletics have a laugh at an Old-Timer's game. Paddy Livingston is at bottom right, but who are the others? Is that Harry Krause at top center or is it Jack Coombs? Perhaps Krause is the fellow at far left? And who is that at the upper right? While each and every one of them had long since retired from the big leagues, a real Old Timer and their former manager, Connie Mack, was still going strong in Philly! The tobacco cards are from the 1911 T-205 set.

Babe and the Yanks gather 'round and listen to hurdy-gurdy music as they enjoy a relaxing moment at spring training in New Orleans, March 15, 1922. It was on this very day that Ruth was named captain of the Yankees, while just a few days earlier, he had signed a contract worth $52,000 a year. As Ruth noted, "I've always wanted to make a grand a week." Despite giving him the big money and added responsibility, the Yanks were well aware that Ruth would be out of action for the first six weeks of the season. He had earlier been suspended for illegally barnstorming with Bob Meusel (third from left) after the '21 World Series.

OUR FRIEND, "OLD SOL," IS ON THE JOB,
AS ALSO IS THE "FUTURE COBB."
"J. PLUVIUS" WILL HAVE A BANNER YEAR,
THE "CHARLEY HORSE" HAS BROKEN LOOSE,
THE ALIBI IS NOW IN USE
WHICH INDICATES THAT SPRING IS DRAWING NEAR.

THE CLUBS ARE ALL IN DIXIELAND,
AND FROM THE DOPE WE UNDERSTAND
THERE'S NOTHING THERE BUT FIRST DIVISION TEAMS.

AS SURE AS 8 GOES INTO 4
THE TAIL-END TEAM WILL BE NO MORE,
AND EVERYBODY'S HAVING PENNANT DREAMS.

THE VETERANS AND YOUNG RECRUITS
ARE PRACTICING DECEPTIVE SHOOTS,
AND EVERYBODY'S HAT IS IN THE RING.
THE SCRIBES ARE SPREADING ON THE SALVE
AND THAT'S HOW IT COMES WE HAVE
A FLOCK OF PENNANT WINNERS—IN THE SPRING.

–L.C. DAVIS, *The Sporting Life*, 4/6/22

THE BASEBALL TEAMS GO SOUTH IN SPRING
TO BASK IN TROPIC WEATHER
AND REVEL IN THE ZEPHYRS OF
A BALMY SOUTHERN SHORE.
AND WHEN THEY BEAT IT NORTH AGAIN
AND HIT THEIR NATIVE HEATHER
THE FRIGID BREEZES WALLOP THEM
AND CHILL THEM TO THE CORE.

IF I POSSESSED A BASEBALL TEAM
I'D SHUN THE TROPIC WEATHER
I'D TAKE 'EM UP TO GREENLAND WHERE
THE ARCTIC BLIZZARDS ROAM.
THE BRACING AIR PREVAILING THERE
WOULD MAKE 'EM TOUGH AS LEATHER,
AND THEY WOULD FEEL LIKE PLAYING BALL
WHEN THEY CAME MARCHING HOME.
—*GEORGE E. PHAIR*
The Sporting Life, 4/14/21

Right, Ducky Medwick (at far left) spends some time relaxing at Sloppy Joe's Bar, a famed night spot in Havana, Cuba. Facing page top, Jay Johnstone, Rick Sutcliffe, and Steve Garvey engage in a rather unorthodox form of training at Vero Beach in 1981. And facing page bottom, in the shade of his sombrero, Hugh Casey enjoys a siesta during spring training in Ciudad Trujillo (now known as Santo Domingo) in the Dominican Republic. No doubt the Dodgers' ace reliever was worn out from the numerous trips he had made from bullpen to mound.

Lou Boudreau put it best when he said: "On Opening Day, the world is all future, no past." Here's a glimpse at the hopeful Opening Day festivities of a couple of Senator ball clubs, below and facing page.

Here, President Truman, a natural southpaw, throws out the traditional first pitch of the season, April 18, 1950. Moments later, Harry tossed out a second ball . . . this time right-handed! Joining in the fun are (left to right) his daughter Margaret, his wife Bess, Harry, Brigadier General Robert Landry, Connie Mack, Vice-President Alben Barkley and Bucky Harris. The Senators defeated Mack's Athletics, the president won a $1 bet, and Washington went on to another second division finish.

A floral wreath, left, wishes Sacramento "Success" on Opening Day at Moreing Field, 1924. Following the club's 112-87 record and second place finish in 1923, the '24 Senators were understandably optimistic about the coming season. But the visiting Vernon Tigers (and Frank Shellenback's spitball) rained on Sacramento's parade, as the Solons fell 7-1. Sacramento would go on to lose 112 times (that's as many losses as they had victories in '23) and end the season in the Pacific Coast League cellar..

Of course, Senator clubs didn't always finish in the cellar. Here the Nats raise the '33 American League championship flag, as a trio of bridesmaid Yankees look on. Left to right: D.C. Commissioner Melvin Hazin, Lou Gehrig, Clark Griffith, Joe McCarthy, Joe Cronin, and Babe Ruth.

In early 1976, with the American league champion Red Sox mired in a ten-game losing streak, a radio station in Boston got a bright idea. Why not hire a witch to put a hex on the streak? Enter Laurie Cabot (top left with Bernie Carbo), an instructor in witch-craft at (where else?) Salem State College. The witch flew (via airplane, not broom) to the Bosox game in Cleveland and cast a spell on the ball club and Bernie Carbo's bat. Poof! The Red Sox won in twelve innings, Carbo got a double, and the club went on to win eight of their next nine.

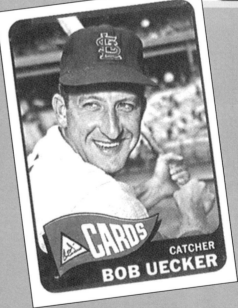

CATCHER
BOB UECKER

As Bob Ueker says: "Ah, those fans! I love 'em." Generally, the feeling is mutual. At left, an excited fan jumps onto the field to person-ally return the compliment to the Athletics' José Canseco, after his 2-homer outburst against the Indians, July 19, 1990.

The Dodger Sym-Phony Band (no, dat ain't dem in da picture) was an institution at Ebbets Field. From their "bandstand" in Section 17, right behind the Dodger dugout, the band would musically mock, deride, and razz opposing players. In July of '51, a mild rhubarb ensued when a local musicians union discovered that one of their members was playing with the Sym-Phony, but not for union wages. Dodger owner Walter O'Malley neatly sidestepped the issue by revamping the band into an all-amateur group. At the same time, O'Malley evidently came down with an acute case of Veeckitis. To accentuate the absurdity of the situation, August 13 was declared "Music Depreciation Night." Even though the game wasn't on the original schedule, nearly 25,000 fans showed up, some 2,000 of whom getting in free as they brought their own instruments! (Now *dat's* dem in da picture).

Cincinnati had Harry Thobe, the Red Sox had Mike "'Nuf sed" McGreevy and the Royal Rooters, Oakland had Crazy George, Wrigley will forever have the Bleacher Bums, just about everyone has had Morganna "The Kissing Bandit," and Brooklyn had Hilda Chester. While Hilda's booming voice was later replaced by her cowbell, she still got the message across. Believe it or not, Hilda had a brief period in which she changed her allegiance to the hated Giants. But the confusion didn't last long and she soon returned to the Flatbush fold.

SPORTING LIFE

5¢

DEVOTED TO

BASE BALL, TRAP SHOOTING AND GENERAL SPORTS

Title Registered in U. S. Patent Office. Copyright, 1910 by the Sporting Life Publishing Company.

| Vol. 55—No. 12 | Philadelphia, May 28, 1910 | Price 5 Cents |

RELIGION OF BASE BALL

Our National Sport Founded Upon the Same Principles As Underlie All True Religion and

ECRETARY JOHN A. HEYDLER, of the National League, hails from Franklin, Pa. In this tidy little town there is published quite a neat and well-conducted paper entitled the "Franklin Evening News," of which Mr. James B. Bosland is managing editor and Mr. E. T. Stevenson city editor. The paper on the 16th inst. published an article under the caption, "The Religion of Base Ball," which we consider well worth reproducing in full in the columns of "Sporting Life"—the one paper which stands always for the highest and best there is in base ball, and which has ever taken the great game soberly and seriously as becomes the chief outdoor sport of a nation of nearly ninety millions of people. It is therefore with the greatest pleasure we reproduce this article from the "Franklin Evening News," which must commend itself to all base ball lovers and may, perhaps, afford food for serious thought to many of "Sporting Life's" serious readers:

RELIGION AND BASE BALL.

That which is religion is essential to base ball. Justice, truth, obedience to law, cheerfulness in serving, faith, hope, good will toward those opposing us, action, soul-expression, are all characteristics and fundamental in religion and in base ball. This is true of all sports, for there can be no pleasure in sports where the conditions are not just, where truth is not observed, where there is a lack of obedience to the rules that have been assented to by those having the power to decide them, where there is a surly attitude of mind, where action is lacking and where the self of each player is not expressed. Faith to struggle, hope to inspire are also essentials of the good game. We have seen

POPULAR SPORTS FAIL

for lack of these things. Horse racing, when it had the essentials of religion, which are justice, truth, faith, hope, good will, action and free expression, was popular. It was a good sport, too, and the horses enjoyed it. Gradually, gambling, bribery, ill will and injustice crowded out the self-expression of riders, the justice and truth in the sport, the good will toward horse and man, the faith that cannot live in a "fixed" deal, the hope that abides not where a certain defeat has been bargained for. The tracks are little used these days. Foot ball also, has lost its element of good will and justice to the individual in the crushing and smashing that maims and makes no count of individual bone breaking, and the sport is on the decline. Card parties are not what they might be, for they have become too liable to be occasions of deceit instead of truth, and of ill will rather

JOIN SABR for more baseball fun!

$35/yr. U..S., $45 Canada and Mexico
$50 Overseas, $20 Student
$20 Senior U.S., $35 Canada and Mexico

Membership includes three inspired baseball publications annually.

Write to:
SABR
P.O. Box 93183
Cleveland, OH 44101
or call:
(216) 575-0500

THE SOCIETY FOR AMERICAN BASEBALL RESEARCH

according to popular opinion, of the best country. It is the game that is most dependent upon the best emotions and impulses. The moment the umpire ceases to be what the public considers just is the moment that the joy in the game ends for all concerned.

appearance at the bat in the last inning. There

MUST BE HOPE.

a hope that will make a man enthusiastic to catch a fly ball when it is two rods over a brush fence and falling. It is always the

All Other Essentials to Moral and Physical Welfare and to Rightful Conduct in This Life.

and a poor batter is fanning the air. Base ball players are not silly talkers. If they amount to anything in the league. They do not stay out late nights; they are temperate, loyal to ideals, calm when abused by thousands, silent when the umpire gives the word that takes them, it seems wrongly, from the race they are making for

HONOR AND SUCCESS.

Would it not be a great thing if some preacher in Franklin could have a church made up of members with the qualities of religion and character demanded by a good game of base ball! Would we not all of us, be somewhere near the hearts of God and free from much of earth's sorrow and strife and foolish throwing away of our powers, and foolish gossip and slander and forgetfulness, if, in the ordinary affairs of life we could be just good ball players for God Almighty, the captain of the great game we play while we abide in this existence! If we could stand quietly and wait our opportunity to strike, as do the players of this game; if we could simply step aside when we fail, as do the best batters, saying nothing and finding no fault, hoping for better skill next time; if we could

ACCEPT THE CALLS OF DUTY

for us to make a sacrifice play, as do the men who make base ball games the wonder of the world, knowing that in the private records of the great Captain every sacrifice is counted in the estimate He makes of what we are; if we could play the center field place, as well as the catcher's, and with as much enthusiasm, in the game of banking, or love, or farming, or housekeeping! These base ball virtues, these principles of true religion, would save the world, would save us, even as they refine and develop and make glorious the souls of the good players who with ball and bat purify themselves and make strong their every power, that on the moving field before the thousands and their own consciences they may not be found lacking. The secret of the success of base ball is that it is

ON THE SQUARE.

The game that is bought or bargained for will destroy the nine, or the league, were it once even hinted about in the homes of the people. The games that we play best in this life, those we win, are, every last one of them, if they give us any real good, won also "on the square." "Easy money" is not a source of happiness. The girl deceived into a marriage she would not make if honestly treated does not make the faithful and helpful wife. The business built up on sharp practice must be paid for by soul agony, as well as mental or physical toil. That element which makes the freshness of the dawn, the pure, sweet touch of the wind, the joy of happy children, the charm of girls that shyly smile on those they love, the gladness of happy